Songs of Idleness

Songs of Idleness

COLLECTED POEMS

B. J. Sadiq

Foreword by Peter Oborne

RESOURCE *Publications* · Eugene, Oregon

SONGS OF IDLENESS
Collected Poems

Resource Publications
An Imprint of Wipf and Stock Publishers
199 W. 8th Ave., Suite 3
Eugene, OR 97401

www.wipfandstock.com

PAPERBACK ISBN: 979-8-3852-5289-3
HARDCOVER ISBN: 979-8-3852-5290-9
EBOOK ISBN: 979-8-3852-5291-6

08/20/25

Cover photograph by Urooj Burhan. Image copyright 2023.
Author photograph by Angelo Calianno. Image copyright 2024.

to my beloved wife, Urooj
and to Fury and Homer,
my pets who spoil me beyond all scales of decency,
and without whom this work should have been
in print much earlier.

"A poet is, before anything else, a person who is passionately in love with language."

—W. H. AUDEN

CONTENTS

Foreword by Peter Oborne   ix

Oh Dear Little Beetle | 1

There was Poetry in the Scene | 2

Proelium | 3

An Autumn Morning at Hughes Hall, Cambridge | 4

It was February Noon and Cricket was on the Breeze | 5

Golden Duck | 7

Ode to Viv Richards | 9

An Ode to Pakistan Cricket | 11

Ode to Sir Garfield Sobers | 14

Sunset in Nathia Gali | 16

Death | 17

On Virtue and Vice | 18

Non est meretrix | 19

I Know where Heaven Lives | 20

Ode to a Lover's Muse | 21

Dr William Brydon's Ordeal—Afghanistan 1842 | 23

My Home is in Autumn | 25

An Elegy written for a four-month old child | 26

Memories from King's College, Cambridge | 27

The Last Call of Kauai (A Hawaiian male bird gone extinct in
    1987) | 28

I Whistle and Hum | 29

Lines Written for Homer my Kashmiri Hound | 30

Business Girl | 31

Platonicus amor | 32

The Hound of Malot | 33

CONTENTS

Camping with my dogs and Bernard Shaw | 37

Early Summer in Bhagwal Village, somewhere in Punjab | 38

Ode to Khushwant Singh | 40

I Got up This Morning | 41

I Have a Quiet Room | 43

Ode to Cambridge | 44

By the Light of the Failing Noon | 45

In Memoriam—My Late Father Javaid Sadiq—I | 46

In Memoriam—My Late Father Javaid Sadiq—II | 48

After Grief | 51

I Heard the Koel's Hum | 52

I Think I'm Dead | 53

On the illness of my Muse—A Satire | 55

Farwell to Her Majesty the Queen | 58

A Breath from the Land of Graves (For the people of Gaza) | 60

Nuclear War | 62

About the Author | 65

FOREWORD

NOT MANY CAN MANAGE decent prose. Even fewer can write a decent poem. B. J. Sadiq can do both. This makes him an all-rounder, a literary equivalent of Garry Sobers or Asif Iqbal. His biography of Imran Khan, a masterpiece of outrageous contemporary biography, proved that political non-fiction can grip like a thriller. With this volume he proves that you don't have to be a professor of English to read poetry.

BJ is not, thank goodness, a modernist. He does not show off. He aims to entertain. Some poets intimidate readers by showing how clever they are. BJ turns his readers into friends. He shares their enthusiasm makes jokes, possesses a sense of rhythm and delivers a natural authority on the page.

Above all he chooses accessible subjects. We too share his love for as well as frustration about Pakistan. We too know the feeling of not being able to get up in the morning. We too are befuddled by cricket.

A great deal of poetry has been written about cricket. Too much. Most of it is lower middle order stuff. BJ's cricketing output is fit to open the batting for any team, and bears comparison with the best cricket poems ever written.

Think of Harold Pinter's

"I saw Len Hutton in his prime / Another time / another time."[1]

Or Alan Ross' "Test Match at Lords":

"Bailey bowling, MacLean cuts him late for one.

I walk from the Long Room into slanting sun."[2]

1. Harold Pinter, "Poem," in *Collected Poems and Prose* (New York: Grove, 1991), 51.

2. Alan Ross, ed., "Test Match at Lord's," in *The Cricketer's Companion* (London: Eyre & Spottiswoode, 1960), 531, lines 1–2.

BJ's *Ode to Pakistan Cricket* can survive and flourish in this heady company. Take these lines:
> "I speak with a heavy heart, and I hope you understand,
> That all is not well, not well in my land."

I would even suggest that his work is a distinct improvement on Byron's:
> "Drive o'er the sward the ball with active force,
> Or chase with nimble feet its rapid course."[3]

A major new talent has arrived. This is a cause for celebration. Here is a new voice: confident, melancholy, witty, humane and strong.

Peter Oborne
Award-Winning British Author

---

3. Lord Byron, "Childish Recollections," in *The Works of Lord Byron*, vol. 1, ed. by Ernest Hartley Coleridge (London: Murray, 1918), 92, lines 131–32.

OH DEAR LITTLE BEETLE

Oh dear little beetle,
What do you do on that pew?
Use your flutters, fly to me,
I'd give you a better view.

Oh dear little beetle,
Come and sit on my palm,
I'd screen you from public gaze,
I'd shield you from harm.

Oh dear little beetle,
How vivid is the image of that hill,
Don't you go anywhere now,
Remember, if foxes don't eat you, snakes will.

THERE WAS POETRY IN THE SCENE

By the last rays of an autumn sun,
A bird of native gene,
Pecked on misty grass,
There was poetry in the scene.

I was alone, all alone by myself,
Reading beneath the oaken green,
The bird had fled to a haunt unknown,
There was poetry in the scene.

But then I saw a lissome girl,
Scurry home; so tall and lean,
The LORD had snuffed the heavenly lamp,
And there was poetry in the scene.

Another day had gone by,
And what a day it had been,
I strolled along and had my song, because;
There was poetry in the scene.

PROELIUM

Some fought for pelf,
Some for peace,
Some for malice,
Some for Greece.
Some fought for lust,
Some for land,
But most fought for things,
They did not understand.
Some fought for faith,
Some for water,
Some for GOD,
Or the enemy's daughter.
Some fought for pride,
Some for distinction,
Nearly all fought for a purpose,
For death and extinction.
As ugly as the devil he is,
As virtuous as a man can be,
Yet both arrive at a common cause,
To fight, die and be free.

AN AUTUMN MORNING AT HUGHES HALL, CAMBRIDGE

Often lying on that frosty grass,
I peered through the distant hedges
The gable frontages, the biking lass,
The study tables behind the ledges.
The bursting of the early light,
The autumn leaves above my head,
The nippy air of the buried night,
All life was out of its bed.
A gentleman with a trilby hat,
Sniffing some important book,
On a chesterfield he mutely sat,
Just by the flaming inglenook.
Students shuffling through lecture notes,
Flopping about the scarlet wall,
Tutors hobbling in overcoats,
It was 8AM at "Hughes Hall."

IT WAS FEBRUARY NOON AND CRICKET WAS ON THE BREEZE

It was February noon, and cricket was on the breeze,
And I returned home to Lawrence Gardens.
The birds were still singing in the trees,
Both sheesham and peepal by nature made,
Casting on the pitch their hallowed shade.
I was a boy before, and this sward was always pure delight,
I am bearded now with streaks of white,
It all came back to me like ancient prose,
A mob of rhymes pushing through my nose,
The air of my town was pleasant and kind,
And cricket conspired to stir our mind,
Mighty eagles above us played,
Their aerial talents fully displayed.
The arcaded pavillion of Georgian days,
Screening us all from public gaze,
The wainscotted walls; the elegant pews,
The museum where dwells heroic news,
The gabled walls; the cobbles brown and dry,
And pretty lasses of our Oxbridge Alumni,
Then in walked Majid for old legend known,
Making this site his very own,
In walked he in his stooping grace,
Trudging beside me with downcast face,
His puffed collar; his polished hat,
His speckless whites; his Gray-Nicolls bat,
A national icon; a Cambridge Blue,

Played for Glamorgan; and now playing for us too.
He slashed on the off side; swept on the on,
He did it on merit long before we were born;
He did it to the Holdings; did it to Lillie,
And made all manner of bowling look genuinely silly,
His movements were all marked by grace,
A princely laziness ascended his face.
Those who know him can proudly say,
He routed great teams the spartan way.
And piled runs upon runs with majestic ease,
From Cambridge Fenners to the Pacific seas,
But on this day we couldn't keep our fame,
Though Majid carried his bat yet we lost the game,
All credit to you Oxford; you looked a fine set,
We'd play you again; we're not done yet.
But let us all gather and raise a din,
Because whoever wins today; makes us all win.
We're all one; one honourable band,
Proud of our sport; and proud of our Land.

GOLDEN DUCK

It was a beautiful sunny day,
The birds sat on the trees tweeting,
My flannels were bright; my face was gay,
The bees hummed through the grass fleeting,
I felt my paunch had a lump from too much eating,
Clearly, I'd been too lousy with exercise (had been cheating).

But I'd always known in my heart,
That I'd fetch runs, when the sun's beating,
Batting's no science; it's an art,
Some are born with it; while others are just bleating,
Anyway, I thought I heard the boys chatting:
'The captain's won the toss and we are batting.'

In a trice, I surveyed the pitch,
It had no green tint, strangely tanned, like auburn,
Which stirred in me such an itch,
To clobber the bowlers till they burn.
I dashed in, and following a quick sup,
I put the guard on, and padded up.

Me and the partner both went in,
While he looked in a stupor,
I kept up a confident chin,
After all, I'd been a seasoned trouper.
I looked around the park,
Thinking I should get a ton before its dark.

Though I heard him through his helmet mutter,
'Let me have a go at him my friend',
I turned him the other way in putter,
Bidding him to take the non-strikers end,
To my surprise, the person with the ball was a spinner,
And amusingly looked too young, a beginner.

I took my guard and noticed his wrist,
Turn as though it were a spinning wheel,
Which should have produced a slight twist,
Away from my body, as it shed its seal,
But it was a googly, and through my rump,
Sneaked to dislodge the head of my leg stump.

I heard a gentleman at the fence emit an 'oh'
Followed by a fit of laughter,
I thought I'd head to the pavilion without a row,
Or else there'd be a bigger disaster,
I feel one needs more than just bad luck,
To get bowled out, for a golden duck.

ODE TO VIV RICHARDS

Let me tell you of a man,
In Antigua was he born,
An Isle of Gothic ruins,
And beaches forlorn.

He swaggered on to the field,
And batted in style,
A certain disdainful air he had,
As he danced down a mile.

He'd take his guard in a gruffly way,
And shot at you an unnerving glance,
He'd tap an odd bump on the pitch,
Before settling in his stance.

His chest like a knight, thrusted out,
Protruded was his arse,
He butchered the very best of bowling,
And made it look a farce.

Between his teeth a gum he gnawed,
And perched on his head—a maroon cap,
And milked his runs in such a manner,
As though he were taking a nap.

A fraction wide, and through the covers he flayed,
Too straight, and he clipped through mid-wicket,
I don't think a finer batsman,
Can we ever see in cricket.

AN ODE TO PAKISTAN CRICKET

I speak with a heavy heart; and I hope you understand,
That all is not well, not well in my land,
Like most nations on our little earth,
We've had our troubles since birth,
A country formed on theological basis,
Home to the most divided of races,
Unfortunate men, who scarcely unite,
Unconsciously they always fight,
But sometimes in a dull, dreary night,
When the moon's rimmed with lurid light,
I'd think of our moments of national joy,
Moments I'd enjoy as a little boy,
Moments of common gain,
Of grief, of tears, of loss and pain,
Moments when our own fighting's done,
Gives us cause to fight as one,
Yes sir, there's only one thing that keeps us all together,
A bat made of wood; and a ball made of leather,
Cricket here, is the thing,
It's when we all together sing,
It's just cricket that we all love,
More than the LORD of the skies above,
We simply and truly love this game,
A game that brought us global fame,
A sport in which we're awfully good,
Displaying character of nationhood,
A matter of pride, of integrity, of national grace,

And for that we must thank the English race.
Now, must I allude? If you haven't a clue,
To "The Oval" which was the venue,
And where it all started,
Not sure if you've heard of it before,
The year was 1954,
And our men were direly broken hearted,
With Hanif gone for a duck,
But the weather provided some luck,
And Fazl, in spite of having a sprained finger,
Worked to great effect, his in-swinger,
Hence, the great English side was defeated,
And with such rapture our boys were treated,
Thereafter we became,
So very obsessed with this game,
So obsessed, and I don't lie,
It almost became a national cry,
We played it in the streets, we played it in-doors,
We played it in our villages, and by the shores,
We'd play from the earliest prayer call,
We'd play it with a kookaburra or a tennis ball.
We played it in the mountains, in forests dense,
We played it at the cost of all common sense,
That is; we played all the time,
In summer haze, and in winter's prime,
We played it nearly all the time.
And then followed our years in assent,
On the cricket field I meant,
Because off the field we had ample cause,
To put in place our martial laws,
Or the judges who have since long been aching,

For the pleasures of money making,
But God bless our heroic mothers,
For giving us the four Muhammad brothers,
And may he also bless the Burki sisters,
For one of our most adored Prime Ministers,
I'd say nothing of the man's political career,
But of his cricket; we're all very clear,
He led with discipline; he led with vigour,
He was really, quite a charismatic figure,
With him our cricket came of age,
Our batsmen had class; our bowlers had rage,
If Akram moved the ball both ways,
Waqar had even better days,
If Qadir spun his googlies through the air,
Anwar stroked with an inveterate flair,
If Afridi had his hitting powers,
Akhtar had his miles per hours,
Apologies! My apologies,
For an ode of so great a length,
I wished to write it with all my strength,
And I think, by this time, you have the mind,
To know just how vital, cricket is to our kind,
Our love for the game is truly profound,
It brought us after all, global renown,
A sport in which we're awfully good,
Displaying a nerve of nationhood,
And now in this dull and dreary night,
As the moon's rimmed with lurid light,
And I sit, musing through a noiseless sound,
I think I am eternally bound to a cricket ground.

ODE TO SIR GARFIELD SOBERS

In the summer of 1954,
When young Sobers was lithe and seventeen,
With no magical score,
Yet to his credit, (which drew a sudden spleen),
In his coaches, who knew batting at six or seven,
Should neither help the lad, nor his playing eleven.

But as the boy moved up the order,
To finally settle at number three,
And genuinely began to bother,
With strokes through the covers and off the knee,
Besides he were a thinking sort of spinner,
And when placed in the gully, proved a winner.

Though it was not until the year 1958,
In a game against Pakistan,
That he saw the coming of his fate,
At Sabina Park, by the barn,
Where Hanif had already tested the bowlers to their limits,
That is; occupying the crease for 15 hours and 10 minutes.

It was the third day of play,
The Windies were one down for eighty seven,
As Sobers swiftly made his way,
And timed the ball to such perfection (it was purely heaven).
His partner on the other end, Sir Clyde Walcott,
Saw the hapless bowling yield to an onslaught.

He milked his runs, as though having a banter,
And in the process came within reach,
Of Hanif's 337, (which at a canter),
He did manage to breach.
In came Hanif with the bowl, agreeably narked,
But Garry dispatched him to a corner he'd marked.

His batting style was exceedingly inviting,
The high back lift, the supple feet,
All made for a very pretty sighting,
Perhaps there'd never been a cricketer so complete.
One better than even Bradman; yes it is just,
Of me to say, the man was formed of superior dust.

SUNSET IN NATHIA GALI

Every plant that drinks the morning dew,
Every cloud that through these mountains sail,
Are mere panegyrics to the skill of GOD,
Who never strives, and never fail,
Let my numbers please the feathered throng,
Let him who hears applaud my song,
In his heart eternal wisdom reigns,
Himself unseen, yet his mark remains,
Kind on the muse are these verdant bowers,
Such a world she weaves in my silent hours,
Sunsets like souls never die,
In the stroke of a painter they live; in the lays of a poet they lie.

DEATH

A little bird, newly born fell from a ledge
in a bole, down into a brushwood hole.
Just by the hedge.
Two pups scuffled over her organs.
I picked up one of them,
and the bird slipped out of the jaws.
Like running water.
All nerves, crying for God's name,
No help came.
Her mum saw the feud from her perch,
and raised a racket.
I put her on a wall crawling with creepers,
her breathing was a torment.
A drop of water might have brought
her relief.
But her shock was brief.
I saw her little eyes click open,
as though saying: 'it's ok, I can do this; I am almost there.'
And then the pups creeped out of a grassy lair,
And began to brawl.
The bird had paid a heavy price,
I buried her, she was cold as ice.

ON VIRTUE AND VICE

Virtue they say is its own reward,
And should be paid well for its trouble,
But whatever be its worth,
Vice forever pays double.

NON EST MERETRIX

It was dark,
Where we'd been sweating all night,
She looked raddled, and I, as gay as a lark,
On the table beside laid a fag,
Half-puffed in a flight,
To her pallet where I waited,
With fresh flames of desire, unabated,
And on the edges of the curtains burst the outside light,
Sun was up,
Her powdery form emerged once more,
Out of the deep darkness of her room,
I told her she's not a whore.
I told her I am not like them,
She looked at me, and then stared above,
I said once more, that she's not a whore,
And I come for love.
Her muzzle carved up a smile,
The sewerage pipe, shrieked,
In the next room, a settee squeaked,
We chortled; someone in the flat was taking a leak,
We kissed, and then the bed beneath us creaked.

I KNOW WHERE HEAVEN LIVES

I saw a little girl,
A little girl saw I,
The rain pattered her clothes,
But she couldn't let the pup die.

It was winter,
Cold, killing, yet a work of art,
And if there was a place like Heaven anywhere,
It was in that little girl's heart.

I now know where Heaven Lives,
I saw it from just six feet apart,
When all the world burns like hell,
Heaven breathes in that little girl's heart

ODE TO A LOVER'S MUSE

A little bird cheeped in my ear,
The morning light crept through a space,
And I sat for hours by the sedge,
Of a pretty field, my face,
Swept by the splendours of the sun,
And the whistles of the soft air,
No sound of human dross,
Not a soul anywhere.
But a thing unusual came to pass,
I trust not my eyes that saw,
Twice ten feet from me sate a lass,
Thinly clad, blithe, I gazed in awe.
Springing breasts, half bared,
Limbs tucked in a skirt, fair feet,
Was enough to have the whole of me,
On the edge of my seat.
I leaned forward, to have a closer peek,
At her mien, so full of sun,
And discerned she could hardly be,
Between eighteen and twenty one.
No symptom of corpulence,
Yet ascended her frame
Frail, dark, long ambrosial tresses,
Told her future, a charming dame.
Her eyes made intercourse with the world,
Her lips steeped in red,
Purloined my muses,

And recovered me from the dead.
I laid flat on the ground,
Bitten by cupid's storm,
Thinking the girl could be,
The sun in a human form.
At once returned the muse,
From a moment in sweet exile,
Found me and the muffled breeze,
Alone for a quarter mile.
I long to see once more, what I had seen,
Those beaming eyes rolling in emerald green,
Ah that smile! Sweet odours, transient light,
A gem veiled from all mortal sight.

DR WILLIAM BRYDON'S ORDEAL—
AFGHANISTAN 1842

At the height of the British rule,
Under Elphinstone—a Major General and a fool,
A band of white soldiers in khaki dress,
Fought for newer passages with no egress,
Where unfriendly winds bowed in a rush,
To snowcapped peaks of the Hindu Kush,
But little they knew that those trackless tides,
Were home to deadly Afghan tribes,
Where boys as little as a female breast,
Toyed with matchlocks, in playful jest,
Where all talk by the night fires bore,
Tales of war and the English gore,
They clashed their pulwars, roasted their kill,
Or plucked the Sher Mahi from a Kabul rill,
They'd played since long with hostile thrones,
Wielding heavy pikes with ulnar bones,
The English thought they could abuse them,
Make slaves of their men and use them,
Make whores of their wives,
And mould their boys for European lives,
And have them babble English and brag,
The great charms of the British flag,
But motivations of an imperial eye,
Stirred the bile of a Barakzai,
Ah those ambitions of a puerile queen,
Sent her troopers to an ordeal unseen,

And thus it was; on those treacherous courses,
Our fallen men and their horses,
Threaded through the passes,
Vying for Jalalabad, fearing for their lasses,
The morn appeared commingling with the snow,
Leaving them open to the stings of their foe,
The Afghans laid doggo, waiting to strike,
Upon icy cliffs as a turnpike,
They girded them on rocky grounds,
Took them with muskets; tore them with hounds,
But in the sound of that great fusillade,
The English plodded on with their brigade.
Till one by one on that stony main
They all fell helpless to the Afghan stain
But one Mr Brydon—a Scot,
A surgeon by vocation, stood guard and fought,
Though in the art of soldiery he were dull,
Meaning he almost entirely lost his skull,
Yet he survived somehow the Aryan spleen,
By a copy of the Blackwood magazine,
That he'd squeezed inside his hat, and fled for his name,
In partial anger, and in partial shame,
On his breathless horse he journeyed many a yard,
To reach the walls of Jalalabad,
Babbling of his ordeal, blind with tears,
Vowing never to return in future years,
His horse when put in a stable sighed,
And a few moments later, he died,
Imprimis, William wasn't the lone survivor of the wreck,
Mr Banesse, the Greek merchant trailed him on the trek,
Besides, a handful of Indian havaldars arrived weeks later,
Stuttering tales of that horrid amphitheater.

24

MY HOME IS IN AUTUMN

Through the pines the breeze is blowing,
The squirrel scuttles up the bole,
I scrunch the falling leaves underfoot, knowing;
That summer's over; it's going.
Autumn's in my nostrils, and in my garden I stroll.
My home is in autumn,
That is where I write,
I am tired of endless sunshine,
And a windless night.

AN ELEGY WRITTEN FOR A FOUR-MONTH OLD CHILD

It doesn't know, the dread of dying,
This innocent bud, who never bloomed,
Lives cut short in truth, are blessed,
And those who live too long, are often doomed.

I do envy though the tongue,
Gone mute before his time,
He never knew of love, and loss,
Nor had any sense of crime.

MEMORIES FROM KING'S COLLEGE, CAMBRIDGE

That little pew at King's,
Half shaded from the sun,
Is where I'd go to while away,
And think of things I'd never done.

I'd listen to the susurration of the trees,
I'd look at the clouds upon the breeze,
The redbreast pealing its songs,
And the chapel sounding its gongs.

The light skiff before me by the wall,
The centipede on the grass crawl,
I saw lovers lay on the sward, curled,
What an honour to be a part of that world.

THE LAST CALL OF KAUAI (A HAWAIIAN MALE BIRD GONE EXTINCT IN 1987)

So dreary and dull sounded he,
Lonely Kauai, the last of his tribe,
Squatting on a bare branched tree,
And then winnowing the air,
With careworn eyes,
To look for love, lost to man's enterprise.
He looked up at the heavens,
Free and wide,
Yet no one seemed to be on his side,
He looked at the ground down below,
And that is how he came to know,
He was the last of his tribe,
No one answered him,
No one heard,
Those woeful melodies of a woeful bird.

I WHISTLE AND HUM

The heat's baking; and noontime's dumb,
Yet I whistle and hum,
A ruined man, have I become,
Yet I whistle and hum,
Comforts of this life? I don't have all,
I do have some,
Therefore, I whistle and hum,
I was like a boy reared in shade,
They shaded me, my dad, my mum,
My life now is sunless and gray,
But look! I whistle and hum.

LINES WRITTEN FOR HOMER MY KASHMIRI HOUND

I never thought of writing about him,
One who's usually an arm's length away,
Such a part he plays that without him,
I can never start my day.

He wakes me up with a nudge of his paw,
And sits and waits, just two feet apart,
And beams at me a most faithful smile,
That pierces my breast and melts my heart.

I ramble down to the lounge,
By lack of care, my beard overgrown,
I warm myself a cup of tea,
And fling at him, a frozen bone.

We dress, we wander out, Sunday's in the air,
A sweet melody shoots up from a lark,
I park myself on a dew pearled pew,
While Homer fiddles with a bark.

BUSINESS GIRL

A young girl saw I, sitting by the kerb,
Of a crowded street,
And at the slightest nod of a passing man,
She sprang to her feet.

Her face had an air of a bride,
But beneath the foul gloss, and the arc light,
I could tell she wasn't happy,
And dreaded the path of night.

I could see she wasn't happy,
Drowned in her smile; her spirit mourned,
And while I spoke with alacrity,
She with hunger groaned.

She lighted up a cigarette,
She looked at my fly,
I knew what stirred in her mind,
But I was shy.

I gave her some money,
Bought her some food,
Half stunned, she asked me,
'Sir! Are you not in the mood?'

PLATONICUS AMOR

My notion of the ideal living is simple,
A bog dotted lawn, sloping down to a lake,
No kins, a dog, some books, cardamom tea and a dimple,
In the chin of my spinster, I'd be honest, I am no rake.
Fubsy thighs, upper bosom thrusted out,
Like an English maiden, duty bound,
From my pointed window, I see her snout,
She thinks of me looking round,
We never touch, we're always modest,
I see her cutting vegetables on her pew,
She thinks of me looking round,
While I weave my billets—doux.
And then we both die, without a word,
Wrapped in our graves, sleeping unruffled in cold, in heat,
With silence all around, save a little bird,
Who trills our tale, and that's how we meet.

THE HOUND OF MALOT

Some years ago, in the valley of Malot,
Whose air was thick with the scent of goat,
And the eyes as far as they could see,
Opened on hills of rare beauty,
And a pleasant mass of village houses,
Flying flocks and pretty spouses,
Free from slag heaps and hooting machines
Screened by woods and sloping greens,
It had youths and maidens skipping on the glade,
No sign of woe their cheeks displayed,
The light of the country—those virgin girls,
Of deep blue eyes and wavy curls,
With birds in the morns such notes they sung,
Plastering on the walls the cattle dung,
Here by a quiet, mucky road,
Our hound held his sorry abode.
Homeless he lived with a limp in his feet,
With gloom in his eyes, and nothing to eat.
And upon his snout the wrinkles told,
He must have been nearly a decade old,
Drearily he looked at each passing man;
A bike, a car, a truck, a van,
Looked at the lot with doleful eyes,
Then cracked a smile; and looked too wise,
Then wagged his tail; and curled his mane,
And rolled in dust but rolled in vain,
The world went on no care it had,

The poor old cur they thought was mad
But one gay morn, in a cheery mood,
A sick old man came there with food,
He saw the state the dog was in,
And something stabbed his heart within,
The man sat near a silent brook,
And gave the dog a cheerful look,
The dog in doubt lifted his head,
His spirit was broken by visions dread,
By yells and squeals of the men in the street,
By bricks they lobbed; or the kick of the feet,
Loud urchins of the town; whacked his snout,
He hid in the drains yet they searched him out,
Years ago, when less tedious life had seemed,
And his coat was sleek; his eyes like rubies gleamed,
And naivety informed him; he can
In moments of panic reach out to man.
But in time he knew this devilish place
Was meant entirely for the human race.
And now he's here by this sloppy road,
Holding on his own; a sorry abode.
But this man skirting by a silent brook,
Shot down at him a tender look?
In all his years there never came down,
So gentle a soul in Malot town,
He sat there awhile, picking his food,
Hot mutton flesh, barbecued,
The hound he gathered was grey and grim,
And while he ate had noticed him,
With that he whistled; a call for the feast,
And the hound had throttled like an African beast,

Tamed in the street, familiar of danger
How could he honour the greeting of a stranger?
Yet from a stranger like that; who would drift apart?
It's the sort of virtue that melts your heart.
For weeks and months, they strayed together,
Up and down in country weather,
Through open fields, and shallow mire,
Through weedy paths and shady byre,
Through ponds rattled by boggy waters,
Where sometimes played the village daughters,
Through mizzling rain and sunlit dew,
Old trails that now to them seemed new,
Camping beneath a spreading oak,
Bound by fate in a splendid yoke,
He'd heave at him a knobbly tinder,
And lobbed some meat, burnt like cinder,
The man it appeared had lived alone,
His bride was dead; his kids were grown,
Two boys who in the city had made,
A life out of a humble trade.
But such is life; all luck is brief,
All joy is fleeting; what's left is grief,
One day the man had fallen ill,
Hushed in his room, lying still,
His two boys from the city had made,
Some time out of their humble trade,
And found their man with wheezing breath,
Slipping into a certain death,
All cures employed to save him failed,
His eyes were puffed; his face had paled,
Outside the poor, homesick dog,

Lay listless, bleached with evening fog,
Starved by the house where he slept,
Thought of his master and inaudibly, wept.
And when the time had finally, finally come,
Bruised and broken; his soul was numb,
The world about him mourned the loss,
Of one who gave his life a toss,
In all his years; there never came down,
So gentle a soul in Malot town,
His kith and line, once all tears were shed,
Left forever for the lives they led,
But the poor hound, so listless and sad,
Had lost the only friend he had,
And of that hound it was fondly said,
That round the dead man's grave, he found his bed.

CAMPING WITH MY DOGS AND BERNARD SHAW

I seek shelter in dark willows,
I lit-up up the logs,
I keep humans at bay,
And go camping with my dogs.

I stare into the darkening night,
The dogs waiting for my word, sit,
They curl up and snore by my feet,
And I dip my nose in Shavian wit.

EARLY SUMMER IN BHAGWAL VILLAGE, SOMEWHERE IN PUNJAB

When over that hill the one that skims the bog land;
And a coppice of dark banyan trees; whose roots coil like skeins,
A golden twilight crawls,
And swallows whatever is left of light,
The sun teases before his final sting,
Waits patiently, like a griddle cooling against the wall,
Shadows extend an inch; mercuries fall;
Dragonflies and peat brown butterflies; burst out from the flax dam,
There is a sense of threat.
More is coming,
Lizards rustle through thorny tracks,
Frogs hop over the water weeds,
Some sail aloft dank moss,
In that field on the edge of the mountain; a kine noses into line,
tenderly chewing its cud.
A tractor rusts away like an artefact,
A tautened village girl, tugs at the udder,
Rubs sleep from her eyes,
Shoves away the flies;
They have her blood in their veins;
She smells of cow dung, curry, and bog-sweat;
And her man trowels furiously with cult-like energy;
Plucks a set of weeds, and slashes at the nettles.
In the flanks; there are arroyos too; some three or four feet deep,
Almost burrowed; where lovers sin and sleep,
Or where wild pariahs sleep out their days;

Or whelp their litters.

Birds cheep a familiar melody; they have an inveterate quality of knowing it all before us.

There is a sound of prophecy upon the breeze,

Upon the moving banyan trees.

A cloudburst; a thunder roar,

And then whispers of a gentle downpour,

The branchy woods will flood;

And new tributaries will emerge in the mud;

and merge with bog water.

Soon the trees will turn pale and brush like from the heat;

And their leaves like darkened nails will fall and fly into the side-streets and by-roads.

Another year will die.

Another year will live.

ODE TO KHUSHWANT SINGH

Old times, when the mind was rather new,
I recall reading him, on our grand Papa's pew,
Novellas, wits, for young and old folks,
A severe impulse too for dirty jokes.
But his short prose was the main clincher,
And the highest point of the oeuvre: 'The Bottom Pincher'.
His 'Train to Pakistan' was bold and biting,
A great addition to the art of novel writing.
I found treasure in his other works, when older,
His pen had the pluck to talk of themes bolder,
A good writer he said is a beast that offends,
Has considerable readership, but very few friends.
And authors with no vice to them turn to rust,
Unless they have a bent for sexual lust,
That should make them immortal; keep them in print,
Even if all they wrote was but for a little stint,
For this and for other reasons, combined,
His critics chided him for a dirty mind,
But he was clear like all free spirited, devil-may-care men,
That if he can't kill with a gun; he'd stain with a pen.
And stain in style and cause a row,
And shake up the walls of the status quo.
His native wit was both boyish and skittish,
Charmed us, the Americans and the British,
To me, he's above all those myrmidons, condemned to scrawl,
Roy, Rushdie and V.S. Naipaul,
There'd be others indeed; but he must remain,
The finest pen ever forged by the Indian plain.

I GOT UP THIS MORNING

I got up this morning,
Rubbing my eyes, lazy,
It was the best morn this winter,
Sun peering, warm, scarcely hazy.

I went to the park,
The grass had picked up frost,
The black pew was wet,
The sparrow flopped about, lost.

A little girl played there,
My neighbour's daughter,
Nibbling milk biscuits,
Gulping water.

A few other men strayed,
One of them, a very old man,
Bespectacled, aquiline nosed,
With grandchildren who in a circuit ran.

One lady, freshly married,
Red lipped, richly garmented,
Caressed her man's mane,
With hands soap scented.

I sat sniffing these views,
I resumed the chapter I started at night,
I read on and on,
Till the sun wheeled to its winter height.

I HAVE A QUIET ROOM

I have a quiet room, all to myself,
A life of mental drudgery that I choose,
Where ancient spirits come and go,
Unlocking a rare treasure: "My Muse."

The room is small, four shelves only,
Housing all from Orwell to Greene,
Plays by Shaw, by Pinter too,
And poetry that's rarely seen.

An arm chair, where in a megrim I sink,
Or when a sudden thought descends,
A silly gadget too within my reach,
To chat with silly friends.

Fellows, if no flair for art you possess,
And nothing of merit in that line you found,
Please keep away for Heaven's sake,
This room for me is "Holy Ground."

ODE TO CAMBRIDGE

Distinguished Cambridge! Ye emblem of knowledge!
There's wisdom in your story,
Your soil is fretted with tales of yore,
Your works are steeped in glory.

Blessed be your gravel paths,
Your river hemmed in by oaks,
Your skies are pricked by lofty steeples,
Your halls are full of important folks.

BY THE LIGHT OF THE FAILING NOON

Through sooty paths and shady,
I went to weave a tune,
For my loyal Pindi lady,
By the light of the failing noon.
And then the Koel heard me too,
And sang till the sky was amber blue,
The usual sprinkle of summer rain,
Had renewed my verdant, thirsty main,
One sniff of my dear old plateau,
The smell of goats and chai,
And peals of "Allah o Akbar,"
Ringing through the sky.
And I went to weave my tune,
By the light of the waning noon.

IN MEMORIAM—MY LATE FATHER JAVAID SADIQ—I

Very easily did we leave him alone,
In that frosty mortuary,
He was there the whole night,
Without bedroom light,
Without his bed,
His pillow that warmed his head,
A day earlier he had life,
And he gave me such hopeful gaze,
That I felt certain that nothing can go wrong,
That familiar fatherly look,
Was that the end of our time together?
The day had finally arrived,
The day as kids we never look forward to,
His front had grown pallid from cancer,
His skin was like clod-clay,
And as it appeared,
His voice had disappeared,
And then the vitals started sinking,
And I stood there thinking,
About him,
Of the life without him,
I thought if there was a way to save him?
If he could outlive the time our LORD gave him?
He then breathed a little mournful breath,
And then sped to his death,
And I, clasped his unmoving palm,

Tried lifting his arm,
Opened his eyes, they were tight,
The beat was missing, they had no light,
It was 8:30, summer night.
I then put him down in his burial place,
Still tapping at his feet, for a little trace,
Of life, but nothing came,
We marked the grave by his name,
I then went to his room,
Pulled aside those magenta curtains,
The smell of his cologne lingered in the air,
I looked for him again; but he wasn't there.

IN MEMORIAM—MY LATE FATHER JAVAID SADIQ—II

I mostly think of my father,
He died in May of this year,
I think of him in the depths of the dark,
And shed a little tear.

He comes back to me,
The minute I slide into my bed,
His white saintly hair,
Jutting round his head.

The moustache, thinly cut,
The neatly ironed suit,
The mole next to his lip,
The sleekly polished boot.

His Anglican manners,
His great pile of books,
His love of Shakespeare;
And his classic thespian looks.

His fondness for the English race,
His loathing of the silly,
His love of Caribbean cricket;
And potterings through Piccadilly.

He enjoyed having a banter,
And kept a trilby-hat,
He rooted for Sir Garry,
As he strode out to bat.

He liked to dine at the Gymkhana Club,
And travelled often by planes,
He loved the nip of the winter season,
And like me loved the rains.

A taste for comfy housing he had,
With lack of comfort, affronted,
A taste for a room with an inglenook,
And a house that was gable fronted.

A taste for a chesterfield sofa,
And a watercolor of a fane,
A rocking chair made of maple wood,
And cutlery of porcelain.

He loved his shopping from Marks & Spencer,
Fondly tramped on Bond Street,
He kept his store of suits and ties,
And printed socks for his feet.

A banker by profession was he,
Aren't bankers a handsome breed?
He lost his gains on our schooling,
And for hoarding had no greed.

City and plain had felt his gain
From Peshawar to the Arabian Sea,
He left his mark wherever he went,
And now he lives in me.

A life without my only friend,
A life in fear so badly gripped,
He'd now live in my heart till death,
And also in this manuscript.

AFTER GRIEF

Where did we go wrong?
I asked myself late at night.
Why did we trample the weak?
Why did we bolster the strong?
I drowned in despair till it was light,
Where the hell did we go wrong?
I then walked alone through the misty day,
By dirty lanes, tuning my song,
And thought my world no longer gay,
Where many a sleepless nights I endure,
Yet fail to find a suitable cure,
I thought of the man who upon us rules,
No better, no worse, than all those fools,
Who came before him as nature's curse,
And milked our labours to fill their purse.

I HEARD THE KOEL'S HUM

I heard the koel's hum,
From my sanctum—my haunt,
I wanted exile,
And stepped out for a quick jaunt.
I perished into the cold,
Into the haze of gold; its color drained;
And renewed those walks of old,
Till it lightly rained.
I saw the wind blow,
And the supple branches dance,
And wherever I'd go,
I slipped into a trance.
Through me a spirit passed,
Nature had more substance;
And it spoke to me, at last.

I THINK I'M DEAD

I think I'm already dead,
As I can't get out of my bed,
I am listless and overwrought,
I try to get up but I cannot,
Nothing's working, neither my partner's care,
Nor the spoor of my animal's hair,
His bark is distant and low,
Is he around me? How would I know?
And strangely my neighbour's not fighting,
Or throwing at me her temper,
Or making a joke of what I'm writing,
Why? Why can I not get out of my bed?
What's all this whirring in my head?
Where's the coolness of my silent bowers?
Where often I'd renew my rhyming powers,
Where are my hills; that drink the summer rain?
And my day's torch, swallowed in the main,
And my nymphs? In whose arms I played?
And where many a glorious verse I made,
I tear my locks; I beat my breast,
I can't hear my voice; I'm sick of this rest,
I shout in my highest note,
But my sound somehow, dies in my throat,
Where are all my books, still unread?
Some lying on my shelf,
And some, by my bed,
Oh GOD! They're everywhere, must I die?

Some in my closet,
Some here, where I lie,
Where's the dimness of my eve?
Where's the freshness of my morn?
Has my soul taken its leave?
Am I on the cusp of a new dawn?
The world I knew was carved in dreams,
But that world I knew has choked, it seems.
I'm convinced I'm dead,
Because I can't get out of my bed,
I wish I had a son,
Or a sweet daughter full of mirth,
To entomb me as my hours are done,
In some verdant spot of earth,
I know, I know I'm dead,
Because I can't get out of my bed.

ON THE ILLNESS OF MY MUSE—A SATIRE

I sat alone, maimed by self doubt,
What came naturally to me, was not coming out,
And I thought myself rather insane,
Making little use of my brain,
That is to say my darling muse,
Was showing marks of illness and abuse,
I'd put her to bed with a hot bottle,
A good supper and a book of Aristotle,
And lit in her room a fine fire,
And brought her all the books she'd admire,
She took her drink and a little she read,
But as reading gave her fits; she went to bed,
I'm much indebted to her long and faithful service,
So naturally, her present profile made me nervous,
The muse had slept for a full six hours,
When a specialist arrived with healing powers,
His fees mind you, is exceedingly high,
But one's got to see ones muse fly,
I paid it, pronto, no questions asked,
And the doctor set to work at last,
He approached the couch where the patient lay,
And sent all the servants immediately away,
And proceeded to question her upon her symptoms,
'Don't you worry I have cured many a stubborn victims,
I cured Mr. Rossetti just before his demise,
Even though I saw no hope in his eyes,
I treated the genius of Mr. Seth,

Who soon after scribbled: "The Golden Gate,"
'The treatment you see does indeed work,
Therefore worry you must not,' said he with a smirk.
I'm sure you've consulted other docs,
No cure is truly orthodox,
This said the physician applying a stethoscope,
Swelled the patient's breast with hope,
Bidding the muse to come,
And attempt a blank verse, or at least hum,
A sweet rhyme to jumpstart,
The nerve that powers her heart,
But she was weak—unable to arise,
To expand, to soar, to haunt (to perform any exercise),
By now the doctor had read,
The pulse that revolted and said,
'You know the letters I have been made to feed on,
Compose of articles in the Daily Dawn,
And some reviews of the latest plays,
Which I'm forced to ogle these days,
And an occasional debate in the parliament,
Is death; it is death for my health I meant,
And some pictures of half-clad girls are always in the offing,
Which pretty much is the last nail in my coffin.'
The doctor took me aside,
And said, 'your muse had nothing to hide,
Eremitical seclusion helps your case; but it's bad,
If you over do it; should drive you mad,
I know exactly what seems to be the trouble,
Her appetite of late's not been noble,
Only to her bed she must be confined,
And be fed no crass literature of any kind,

Consider the company of morning birds; consider listening to
 Mozart,
Shun old addictions; try newer forms of intellectual art,
Try your own tongue; it's not dated,
Critics think you're deracinated,
You see, you need in your breast that ambitious glow,
To write incessantly of the things you know,
Shakespeare's too archaic, I say,
Start with Pope, that should make her day,
Give her some Shelly and Browning to partake,
And try some limericks for humour's sake,
Let leering at women be a past time care,
Even if their lips be rosy; their form be fair,
If any signs of inversion or archaism appear,
I am to be summoned at once my dear,
And once she begins to mutter single lines, tags (all that wealth),
And fine phrases; that's a sign of returning health,
Please allow her to dabble in a language she doesn't know,
As that must put a definite end to her woe.'
He told me such breakdowns are common in this heat,
And in no time our lady should be up on her feet.

FARWELL TO HER MAJESTY THE QUEEN

Peace be to our lady Queen,
Lying still in a handsome steeple,
She sometimes vexed her daughter in law,
And sometimes, her people.

Her family's set-up is much hierarchical,
Her son Charles now wears the crown,
William's got ambitions patriarchal,
And Harry has always, an infectious frown.

Never was I in awe of the lady,
The only thing I liked about her,
Were the corgis whom she loved dearly,
And the Spaniel too, (she won't live without her).

Or him, I can't be sure of the gender,
And used it for the ease of my rhyme
Spare me, I don't wish to offend her,
Family, as they go through a rather testing time.

And though I am no austere in giving my prayers,
May the LORD bless the souls departed,
But aren't these crowns a bit heavy on the taxpayers?
I mean they leave the poor rather broken hearted?

In fact, even democracy's such treason,
And dictatorships were always rubbish,
Both boast an absence of reason,
And breed figures exceedingly uppish.

Or perhaps I just have a mind to vent,
I am sorry should you think me rude,
No income have I, and high is my rent,
So naturally I'm in a bad, very bad mood.

A BREATH FROM THE LAND OF GRAVES (FOR THE PEOPLE OF GAZA)

O Israel! Let me unmuzzle my song,
What may seem right to you, is wrong,
Let me unmuzzle this song of mine,
For boys and girls of Palestine,
You who suffer by death's eternal sleep,
I know it is hard and your wound is deep,
But Marshal on, marshal on Dear Gazan youth!
Those wandering kestrels know your truth,
That LORD above in silence sees,
Treachery of your enemies.
But long years ago from Bokhara to Greece,
When tyrants were kinder, and the world had peace,
When man by man in crisis stood
And things were better if not entirely good,
When Jews and Muslims had a common cause,
And unity was favoured by government laws,
Their wants were few, their dreams were one,
In honest toil, their morns begun,
Now hearts have hardened; and we are stunned,
By ways in which old ties are shunned,
Now no one sits beside the dead,
No one mourns the life they led,
No one heeds their cry for aid,
No one foils the mischief made,
Your streets squirt with pregnant gore,
Your infants perish in sleep,

60

And we, perched on a foreign shore,
Forget our world and weep.
And who shall comfort that lovely bride?
Wailing by her husband's side,
Her husband who was killed for truth
Proud member of the Gazan youth.
All night long when bombs resound,
Your bowers shrink to your burial ground,
So many dead are shroud-less laid,
So many lives go without a shade,
But marshal on, the world has heard,
The Halls of Columbia with scorn have stirred,
Their shouts of ire mount the skies,
They mourn your loss, they mock the lies,
They risk their lives for your cause,
Their honest anguish deserves applause.
They call for freedom; and deny the throne,
Though listless you may be; but you're not alone.
With this O Israel I end my song,
Your crimes have lingered far too long.
Consider then the price you'd pay,
For GOD will surely have his way,
The fires that you by hate offend,
Will haunt you in the very end.

NUCLEAR WAR

Today, touched with sunrise our native larks,
Shoot up from the barks,
Full-faced above both our lands; stands the sun,
We both look one.
The streams are gay, the seas are bright,
And everything else seems just alright,
The sweeping Himalayas as they sigh,
Prick the open cerulean sky,
And up in a steely Karakoram town,
Comet-like snowballs tumble down,
And a wandering cloud, like a drifting sack,
Join others in the pack,
And sails to the south,
Of the country's mouth,
Upon a sweltering, starlit plain,
Promising rain,
The clouds come down as torrents, as sleets,
The waters fill the grottoes, the streets,
The kids are out splashing,
Darting at the wind's lashing,
And the rivers look so pretty and blue,
As the driving rain spatters through,
There's no stink of conflict there,
Only calm in the air,
But leaders of these sorry lands,
As venom of their hate expands,
Have become estranged,

Tomorrow I am told, things get changed,

Tomorrow, nature jeers at our lack of harmony;

What used to be us becomes "you and me,"

As we pull the plug on our civilization,

So much for theories of state and nation,

The missiles in flight shall clang,

Bidding the skies to hang,

Mighty spires of smoke,

Spread over miles in a grisly cloak,

And beneath our weeping sky,

All that lives, die.

The wise amongst us had warned,

Of the effects of nukes; even scorned,

But our crowns swelled with vanity;

Shunning all cries for sanity,

Beastly bombs! Whatever they touch, they fry,

Leaving nothing in our lands, nothing in our sky,

Divided by theology; by culture bound,

What a mess we'd make of our weaning ground,

The rush of the Indus; billeted in our flatlands;

Nourishing our humus and wombs;

Mellowing our mud;

Will run cold with innocent blood,

Such a disgrace, a tangled tale,

The defeat of man on a grander scale.

ABOUT THE AUTHOR

B. J. SADIQ IS a British Pakistani writer, a prolific journalist and an English poet. He is the author of a bestselling biography of Pakistan's former Prime Minister, Imran Khan titled "Let There Be Justice: The Political Journey of Imran Khan," and has also written an acclaimed novella in verse, a satire called "Of Kings and Nobilities." He has been a regular contributor to Byline Times, the Middle East Eye and the Friday Times; chiefly reporting on Pakistan, India, Afghanistan and Bangladesh, and has also written for the Spectator and The American Interest. Born in Karachi, "BJ" as his friends like to call him, was reared in the plains of Punjab and the lush Potohar Plateau skirting the foothills of the Himalayan range—the source of much of his muse; but it was really his distinguished education at Cambridge University that corrupted him. It was at Cambridge where he first cultivated his interest in English literature, and weaned on a regular course of poetry which was both antediluvian and also had a modern ring to it. The decline of rhyme upsets him; and he believes that poetry sans rhyme is like Audrey Hepburn without her smile. "Songs of Idleness" is his first collection of poetry. He divides his time between Islamabad and the UK.

www.ingramcontent.com/pod-product-compliance
Lightning Source LLC
Chambersburg PA
CBHW060423050426
42449CB00009B/2097